1000 SIGHT WORDS THE ULTIMATE VOCABULARY BOOK

PICTURE DICTIONARY WITH SENTENCE

English - Russian

action

действия

Action!

actually

фактически

I actually like strawberry.

adjective

прилагательное

Tell me an adjective to describe this.

afraid

боятся

What are you afraid of?

agreed

согласна

They agreed on music.

ahead

впереди

Who was ahead in the race?

allow

позволять

Did the teacher allow him to go play?

apple

яблоко

Eat an apple.

arrived

прибывший

My plane arrived on time.

born

родившийся

Where were you born?

bought

купил

She bought new clothes.

British

британская

Who is the British monarch?

capital

столица

The capital is in Washington DC.

chance

шанс

Dice is a game of chance.

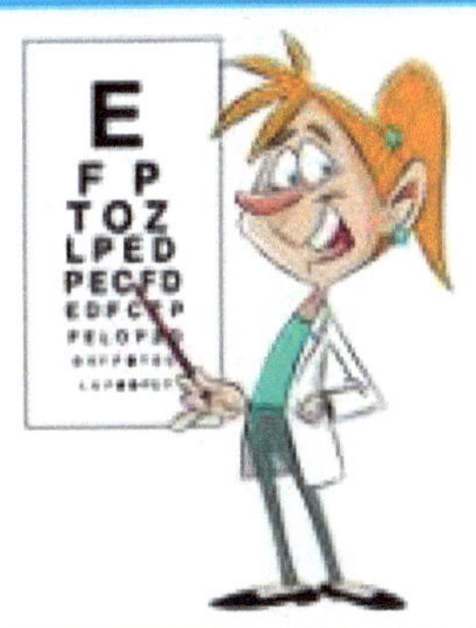

chart

диаграмма

What does your medical chart say?

church

церковь

Did you go to church?

column

колонка

Did you read the newspaper column?

company

компания

What company do you work for?

conditions

условия

What are the weather conditions.

corn

кукуруза

Do you like corn?

cotton

хлопок

A q-tip is made of cotton.

cows

корова

How many cows does he have?

create

создайте

What art did you create?

dead

мертвый

The bug is dead.

deal

сделка

Did you agree on the deal?

death

смерть

The grim reaper is death.

details

подробности

Look for the details.

determine

определить

Did you determine where to go eat?

difficult

сложно

I found this difficult.

division

деление

We did division today.

doesn't

не

Doesn't it sound beautiful?

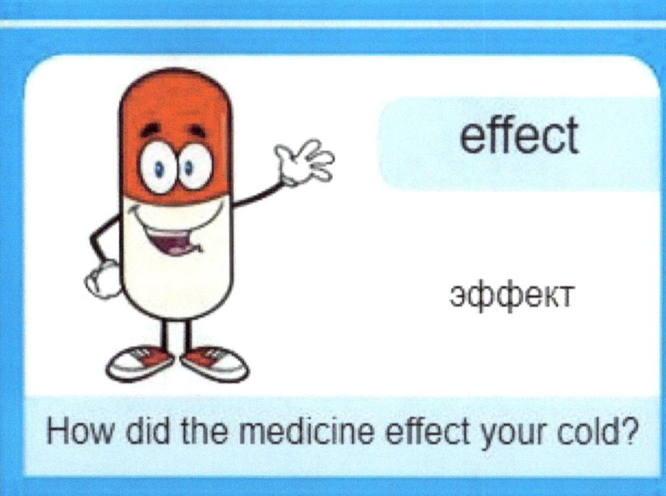

effect

эффект

How did the medicine effect your cold?

entire

все

The entire family was in the picture.

especially

особенный

She especially liked writing.

evening

вечер

The ceremony was this evening.

experience

опыт

She has a lot of experience.

factories

заводы

There are a lot of factories there.

fair

парк развлечений

Let's go to the fair.

fear

страх

I have a huge fear of clowns.

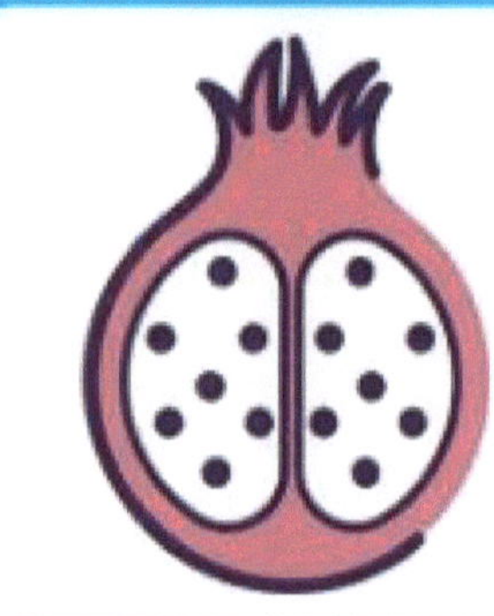

fig

инжир

I ate a fig.

forward

впеpeд

Spring forward the clocks.

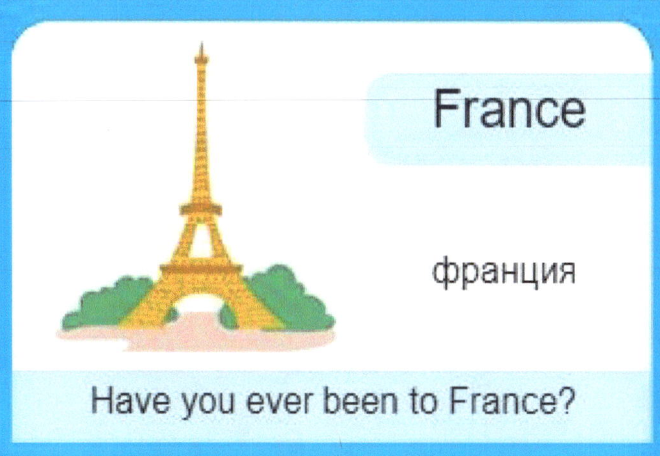

France

франция

Have you ever been to France?

fresh

свежий

All the fruit is fresh.

Greek

греческий

Have you ever had Greek food?

gun

оружие

We played with a water gun.

hoe

мотыга

Use a hoe in the garden.

huge

огромный

Those trees are huge!

isn't

не

Isn't it nice to hang out with friends?

led

лидер

The dog led her.

level

уровень

Use the level to hang the picture.

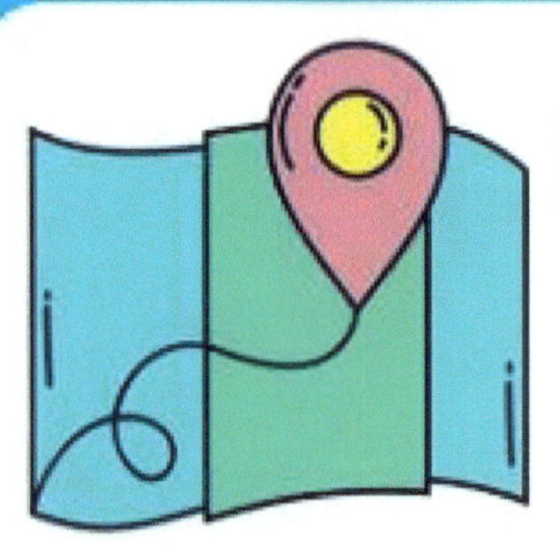

located

расположены

Where is the store located?

march

парад

Are you going to march with the band?

match

согласование

Did you match them?

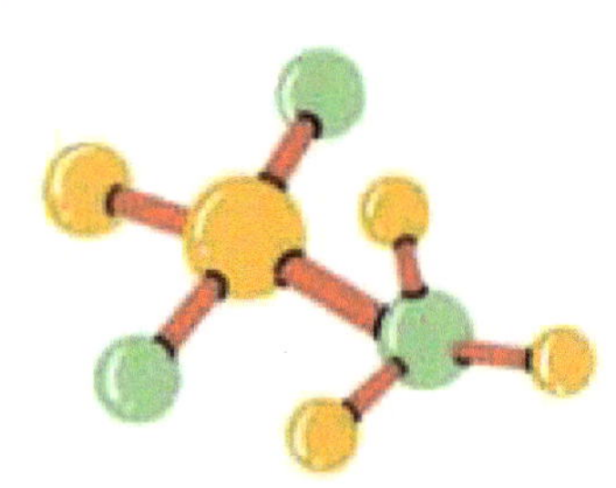

molecules

молекулы

Are those molecules?

northern

к северу

He lives in northern California.

nose

нос

My nose is running.

sir

сэр

Yes, sir!

sister

сестра

Is she your sister?

smell

запах

I love the smell of cookies!

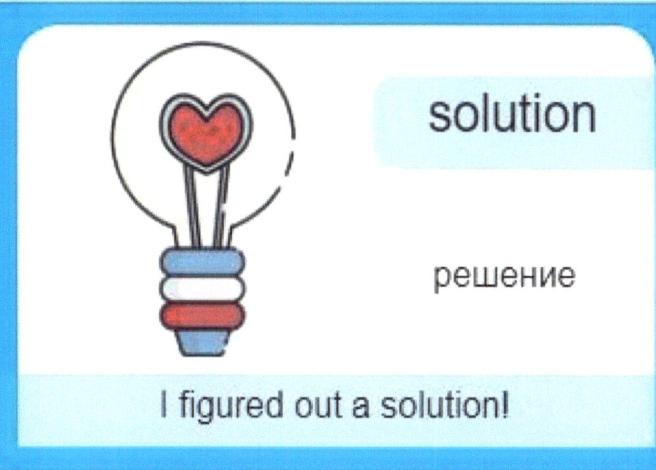

solution

решение

I figured out a solution!

southern

южный

She's a southern belle.

steel

стали

The new building used steel.

stretched

растянуты

We stretched before the workout.

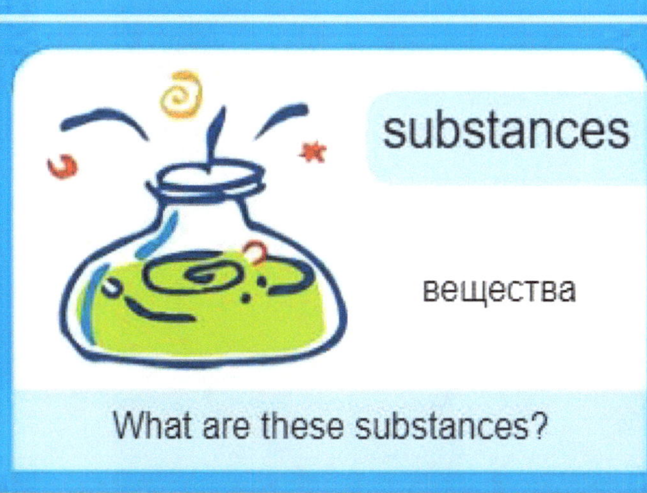

substances

вещества

What are these substances?

suffix

суффикс

What is the suffix of the word?

sugar

сахар

Sugar cube for your tea?

tools

инструменты

May I borrow your tools?

total

всего

What's the total?

track

отслеживать

The runners got on the track.

triangle

треугольник

How many sides does a triangle have?

truck

грузовая машина

Is thaty our truck?

underline

underline

подчеркивание

Underline the word.

various

разные

I watch various shows.

view

посмотреть

That is a beautiful view!

Washington

вашингтон

She is from Washington.

we'll

буду

We'll finish buying our groceries.

western

вестерн

It's western wear day.

win

выиграть

Did you win?

woman

женщина

The woman was on her way to work.

workers

работник

The workers were busy.

wouldn't

не

Wouldn't you like to go shopping?

wrong

неправильно

Did I get it wrong?

yellow

желтый

A banana is yellow.

after

после

You may have dessert after dinner.

again

снова

May we go on the ride again?

air

воздуха

The air was cold.

also

также

I also like baseball.

America

америка

Columbus sailed to America.

animal

животное

My favorite animal is a lion.

another

еще один

Have another cookie.

answer

ответ

Raise your hand to answer.

any

любые

Do you have any crayons?

around

около

Let's travel around the world.

ask

спросить

It's good to ask questions.

away

прочь

Throw your trash away.

back

назад

We went back to school.

because

потому что

I went to bed because I was tired.

before

перед

Sharpen your pencil before the test.

big

большой

The elephant is a big animal.

boy

мальчик

The boy played a basketball.

came

пришел

He came to class.

change

изменение

I save my change.

different

другой

They use different balls.

does

делать

Does he ride the bus?

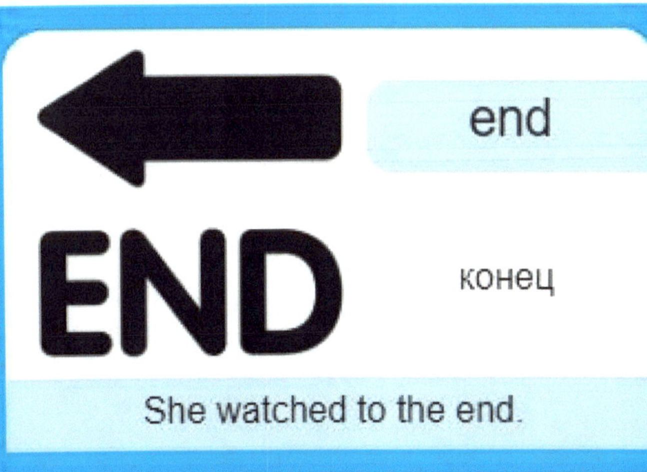

end

конец

She watched to the end.

even

даже

They learned about even numbers.

follow

следовать

Follow the teacher.

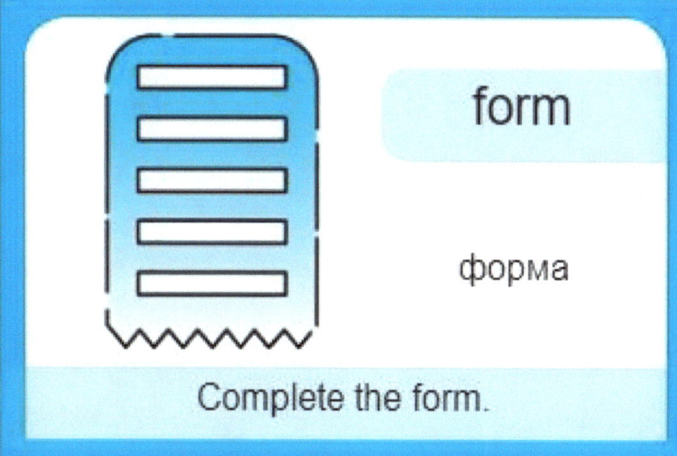

form

форма

Complete the form.

found

нашел

We found a puppy.

give

дать

I like to give gifts.

good

хорошо

The hamburger was good.

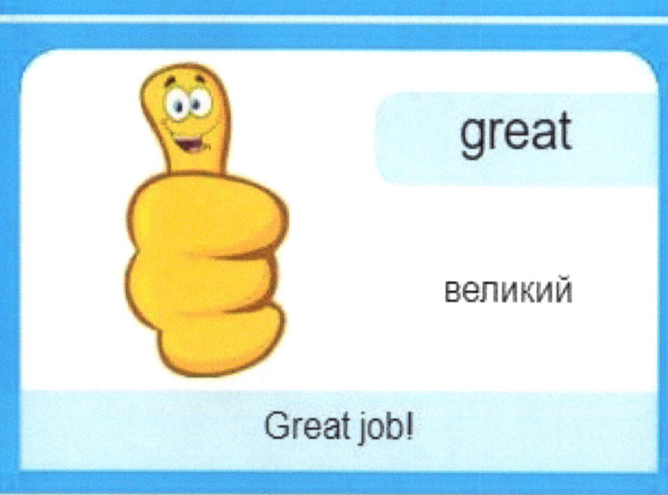

great

великий

Great job!

hand

рука

Please hand in your work.

help

помогите

You should help others.

here

вот

Do you sit here?

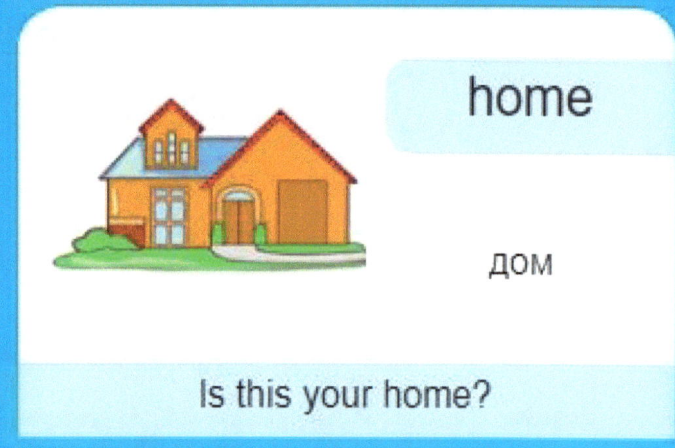

home

дом

Is this your home?

house

жилой дом

The doll house was pink.

just

просто

The train just left.

kind

будь добрым

Be kind to each other.

know

знать

I don't know.

land

земельные участки

They bought some land.

large

большой

A bear is large.

learn

учить

It's fun to learn science.

letter

письмо

He mailed a letter.

line

линии

Please form a line.

little

немного

He has a little sister.

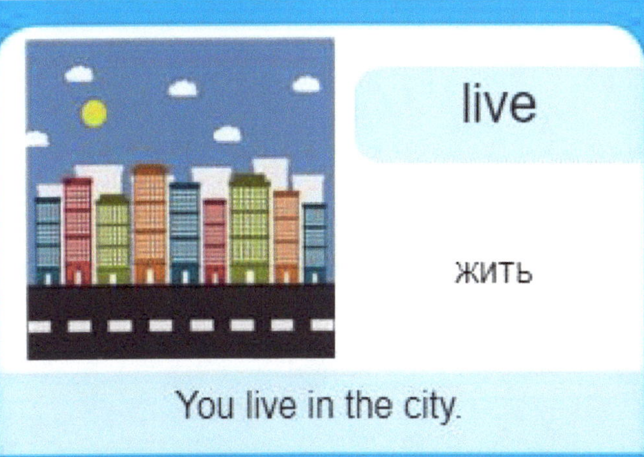

live

жить

You live in the city.

man

мужчина

The man drove.

me

меня

Come with me to the park.

means

средства

She got her by means of a taxi.

men

люди

The men played football.

most

наиболее

Most students like to help.

mother

мама

He loves his mother.

move

шаг

His family decided to move.

much

много

How much is the camera?

must

должен

You must raise your hand.

name

имя

What is his name?

need

хотеть

Do you need to sleep?

new

новый

We have a new teacher.

off

от

The rocket blasted off.

old

старый

Those are old toys.

only

только

There's only one slice left.

our

наш

She was our teacher.

over

над

He jumped over it.

page

страница

Please turn the page.

picture

рисунок

They took their picture.

place

мест

This is my favorite place.

play

играть в

Let's play together!

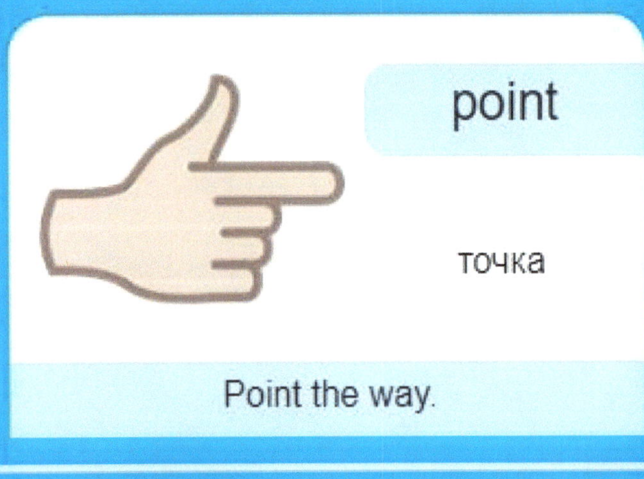

point

точка

Point the way.

put

положил

Please put the supplies away.

read

читать

Do you like to read?

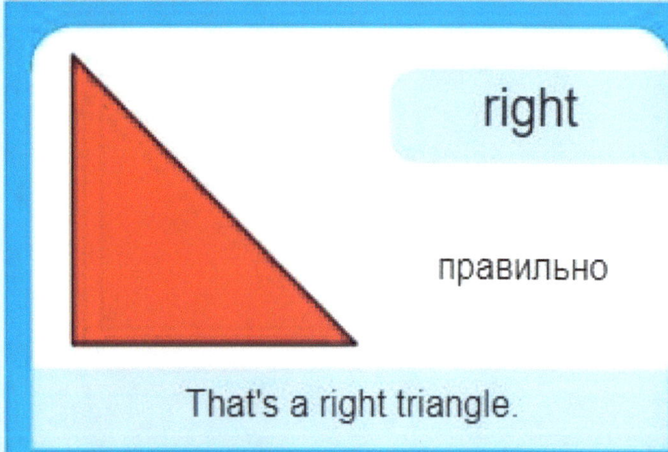

right

правильно

That's a right triangle.

same

одни и те же

Did you get the same answer?

say

сказать

What did you say?

sentence

приговор

Complete the sentence.

set

набор

Please set the table.

should

должен

We should exercise.

show

показать

Show your work.

small

маленький

The ladybug is small.

sound

звук

A bee makes a buzzing sound.

spell

орфографии

Please spell the word.

still

по-прежнему

I still want ice skates.

study

изучение

It's time to study.

such

такие

He is such a good dog.

take

принимать

Please take your seat.

tell

рассказать

She wanted to tell a secret.

things

вещи

She washed a lot of things.

think

считать

Think about it.

three

три

It's the number three.

through

через

He was through with the race.

too

тоже

Do you like chocolate too?

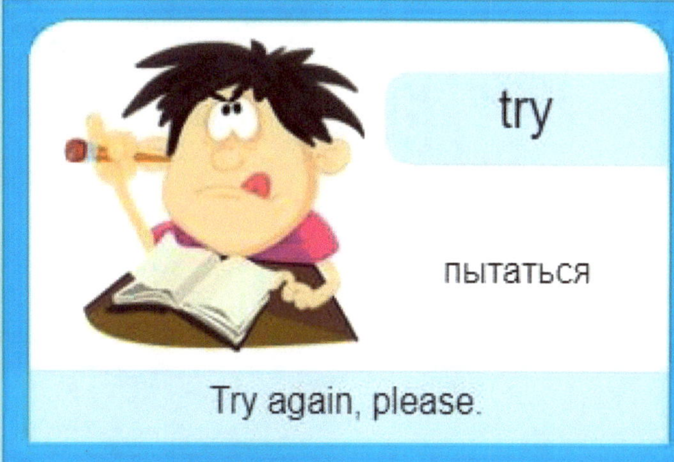

try

пытаться

Try again, please.

turn

очередь

Turn in your homework.

us

нас

She taught us.

very

очень

He is a very good singer.

want

хотеть

I want to ride my bike.

well

хорошо

You did well.

went

пошли

We went to recess.

where

где

Where do you want to go?

why

почему

She asked why?

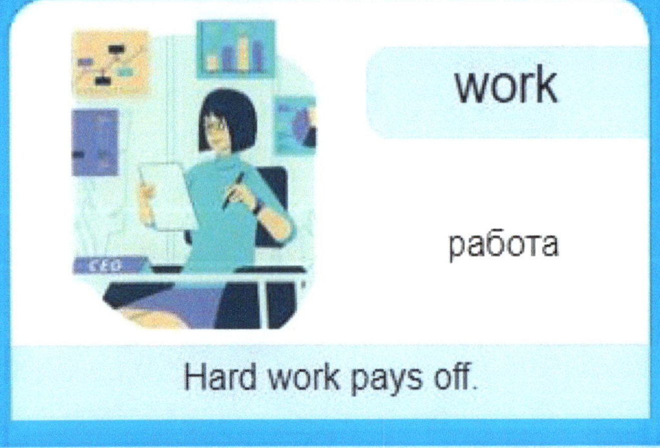

work

работа

Hard work pays off.

world

мир

I want to travel the world.

years

лет

You are five years old today.

above

над

The sky was above them.

add

добавить

If you add one plus two, you get three.

almost

почти

It's almost lunch time.

along

вместе

We get along.

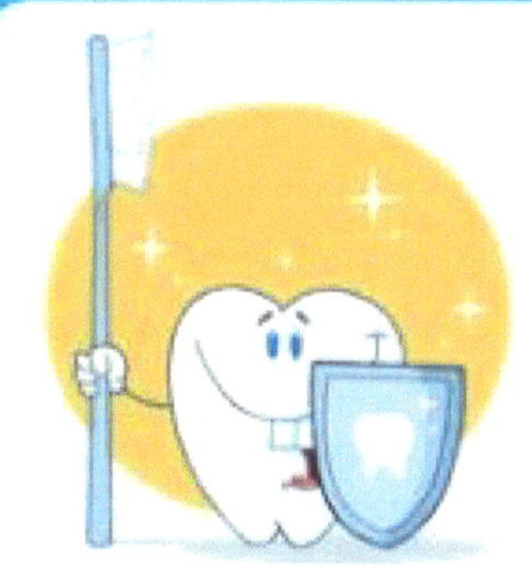

always

всегда

She always brushes her teeth.

began

началось

The baby began to cry.

begin

начать

You may begin your exam.

being

существо

She is being shy.

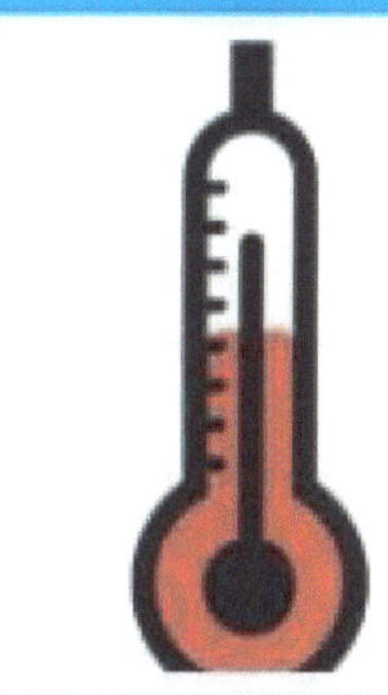

below

ниже

It's below thirty degrees.

between

между

Two is between one and three.

book

книга

I'm reading this book.

both

обе

They both worked on math.

car

машина

He bought a new car.

carry

нести

She had a bag to carry her groceries.

children

дети

Four children sang.

city

город

He worked in the city.

close

близко

Please close the door.

country

страна

Do you live in the country?

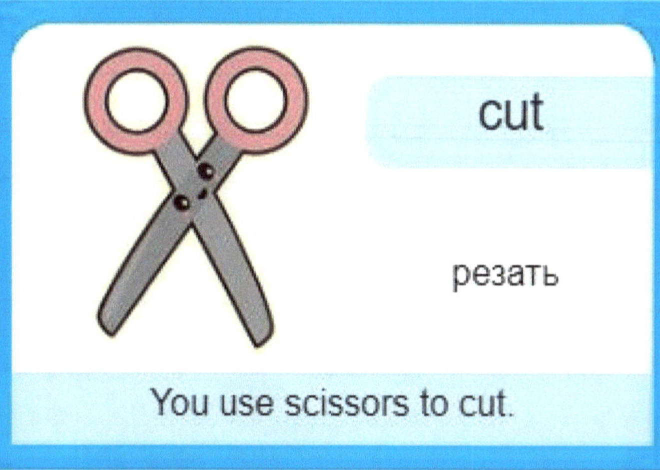

cut

резать

You use scissors to cut.

don't

не

Don't forget!

earth

земля

Our planet is Earth.

eat

есть

I eat bananas.

enough

достаточно

Did you eat enough pancakes?

every

каждый

I shower every day.

example

пример

This is an example of a bird.

eyes

глаза

What color are her eyes?

face

лицо

They were at the face painting booth.

family

семья

How big is your family?

far

далеко

How far is it?

father

отец

Her father walked her to school.

feet

ноги

Put socks on your feet.

few

несколько

She wanted a few more minutes.

food

питание

They made a lot of food.

four

четыре

There were four of them.

girl

девушка

The girl wore pink shoes.

got

получил

She got a hair cut.

group

группа

They were working in a group.

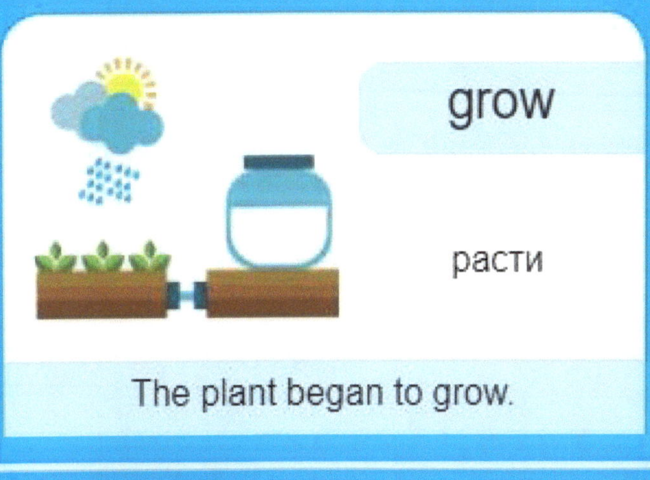

grow

расти

The plant began to grow.

hard

жесткий

He wore a hard hat.

head

глава

He wore a cap on his head.

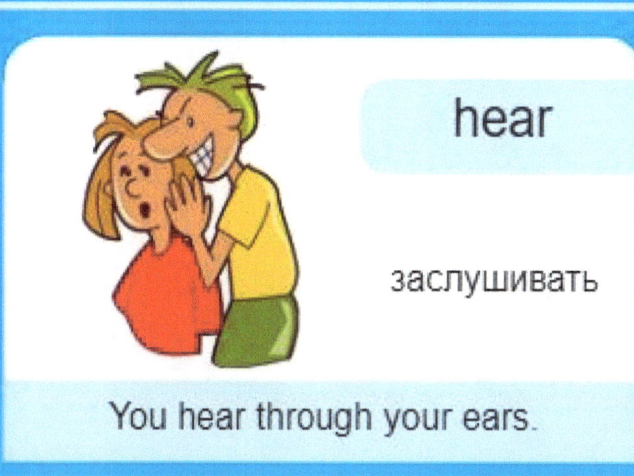

hear

заслушивать

You hear through your ears.

high

высокая

She wore high heels.

idea

идея

I have an idea!

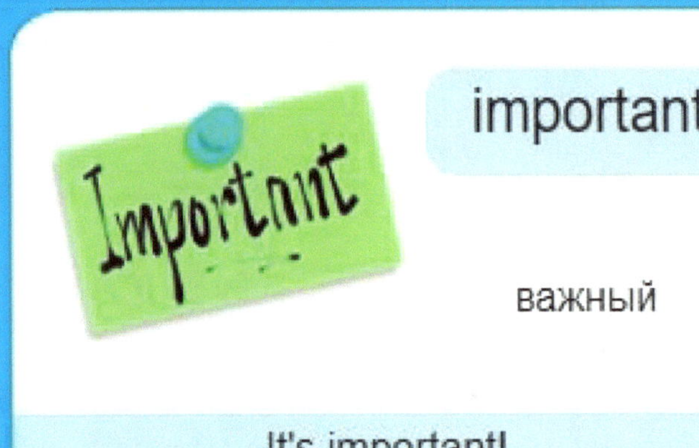

important

важный

It's important!

Indian

индийский

It's an Indian elephant.

it's

является

It's a tiger cub.

keep

хранить

Can you keep a secret?

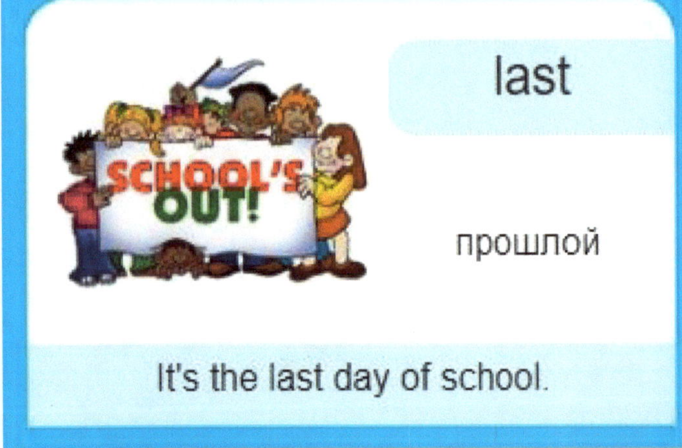

last

прошлой

It's the last day of school.

late

поздно

You're late.

leave

оставлять

He packed to leave.

left

оставил

Are you left or right handed?

let

позволять

Will you let me go fishing?

life

жизнь

Life is about friends and family.

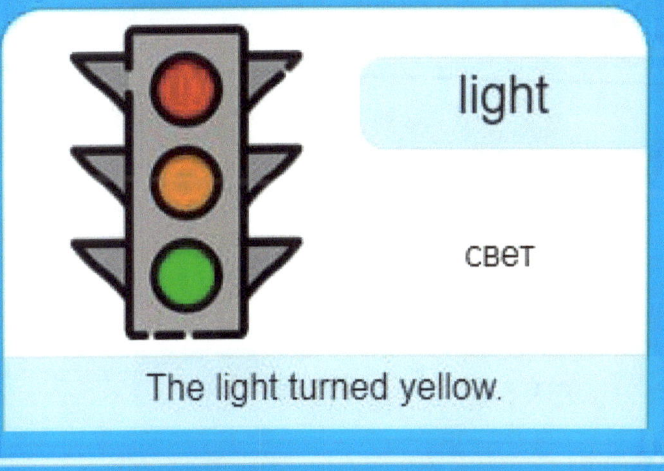

light

свет

The light turned yellow.

list

список

Here's my to-do list

might

мощь

It might rain today.

mile

мили

It's a mile from here.

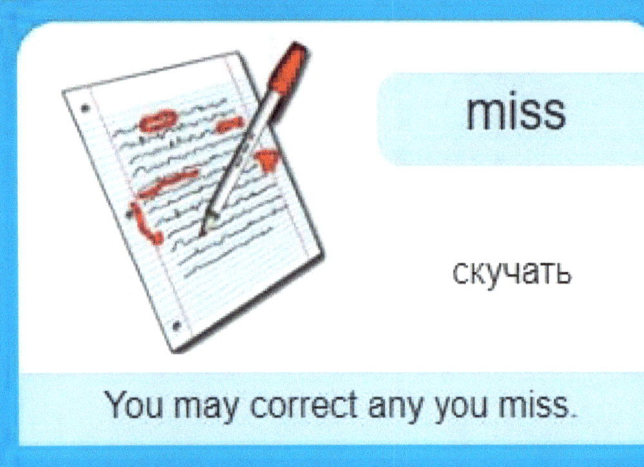

miss

скучать

You may correct any you miss.

mountains

гора

There are alot of mountains here.

near

около

We are near the beach.

never

никогда

I've never broken my leg.

next

следующий

Take the next step.

night

ночь

You can see the stars at night.

often

довольно часто

How often do you watch tv?

once

один раз

Once upon a time...

open

открытый

The door is open.

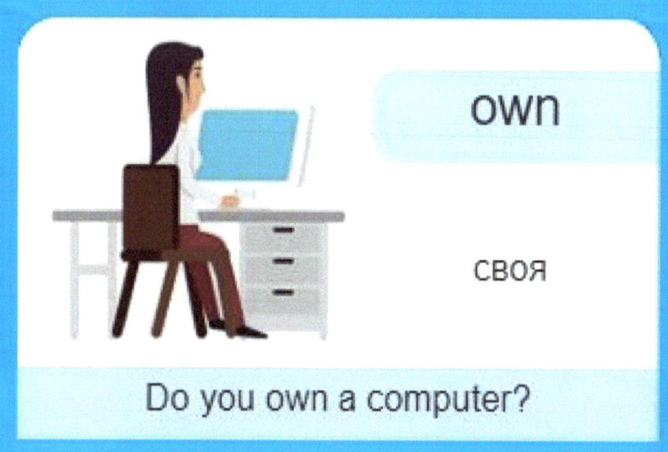

own

своя

Do you own a computer?

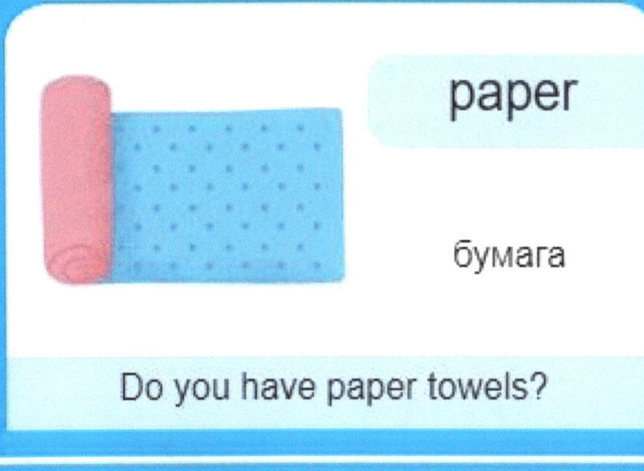

paper

бумага

Do you have paper towels?

plant

растение

I will water the plant.

real

реальный

Her real name is Sally.

river

река

The river is high.

run

запустить

He likes to run with his dog.

saw

видеть

We saw a UFO.

school

школа

Do you like school?

sea

море

The ship is at sea.

second

второй

She won second place.

seem

казаться

You seem busy.

side

сторона

Each side of a square is the same.

something

что-то

Did you hear something?

sometimes

иногда

Sometimes we watch tv.

song

песня

We will sing a song.

soon

скоро

Dinner will be ready soon.

start

начните

Start writing.

state

штат

Which state do you live in?

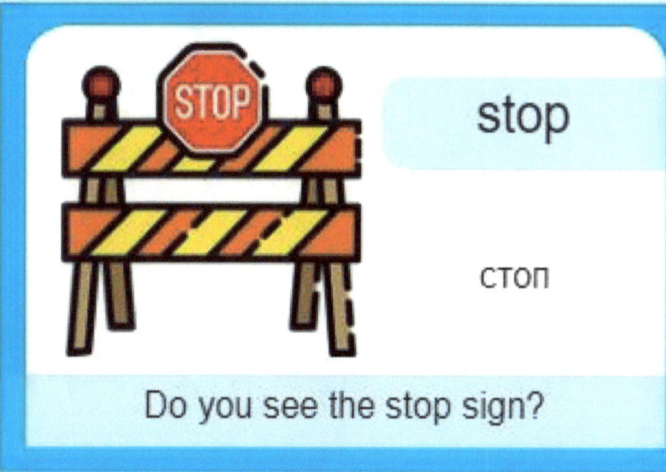

stop

стоп

Do you see the stop sign?

story

история

What's the story about?

talk

разговаривать

Let's talk.

those

те

Those are great cookies!

thought

думал

I thought the novel was good.

together

все вместе

They went shopping together.

took

принимать

He took the last piece.

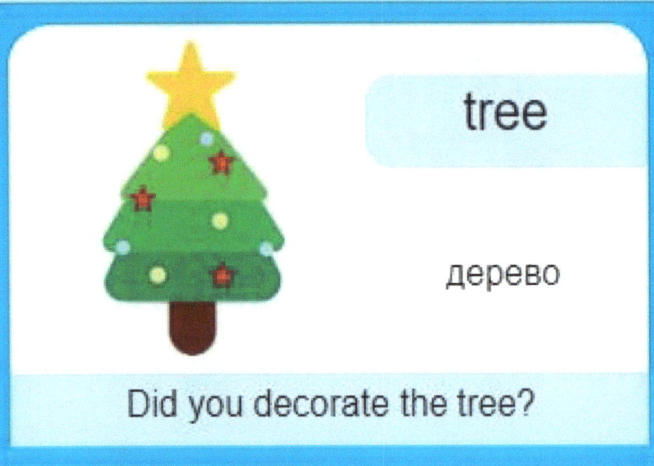

tree

дерево

Did you decorate the tree?

under

под

It lives under the sea.

until

до тех пор

I work until 5 o'clock.

walk

ходить

We went for a walk.

watch

наручные часы

Do you wear a watch?

while

пока

We had fun while skiing.

white
белый

They drew on the white board.

without
без

I can't go without my backpack.

young
молодой

Her kids are young.

across
через

It's across the street.

against
против

It's against the rules.

area
площадь

There are no wild animals in this area.

become
стали

It will become a butterfly.

best
лучший

Do your best!

better

лучше

Feel better soon!

birds

птица

There's a lot of birds.

black

черный

He has a black cat.

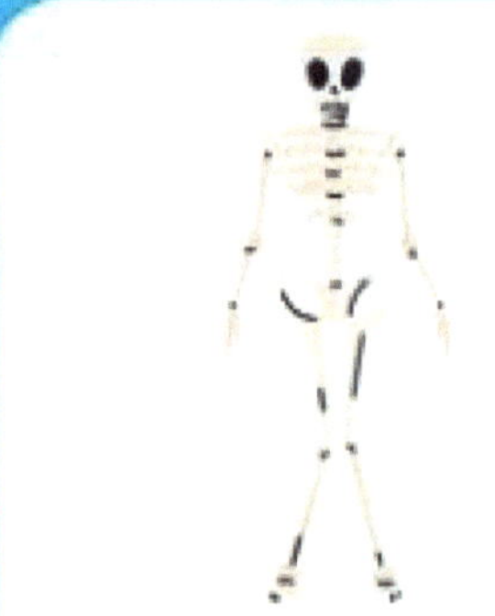

body

тело

The body has a lot of bones.

certain

определенный

Certain words are harder than others.

cold

холодный

It's cold outside.

color

цвет

What is your favorite color?

complete

полный

Did you complete your workout?